"Joy does not simply happen to us.
We have to choose joy and
keep choosing it every day."

~Henri Nouwen

This book was hand-lettered and illustrated by Mary J. DuVal

James 1:2 ~ Whatever Happens, Take It All As Joy

My connection with the book of James goes back to the time I read it as a high school sophomore. One of my friends reminded me that we studied it frequently in our church youth group. I do remember thinking, "This is good stuff!" Even as a youth, I related to the importance of what James communicated as Jesus' teachings about living and I never forgot how helpful I thought it was at that time in my life.

It wasn't until my sister made a comment about a friend of hers that memorized the whole book of James that I decided to pick it up and do a closer reading of it. Because I am an artist, it was natural for me to add drawings to my notes from daily readings. The more I wrote and sketched, the more certain I became that I wanted to share my exploration of the book of James with others.

A 30-year time span between readings (and more life experience!) reconfirmed these gems of wisdom...the kind James speaks of right off in chapter 1, verse 5:

"If any of you is lacking in wisdom, ask God, who gives to all generously and ungrudgingly, and it will be given you."

This is the kind of wisdom that is God-given and life-lived, not world-based and culture-driven.

James does not soft-pedal what goes into an everyday approach to mature living and the reader is confronted within the first few sentences of a verse that should cause a pause in reading and a self-examination of how our personal faith is lived out every day:

"My brothers and sisters, whenever you face
trials of any kind, consider it nothing but joy..." (v2)

If you don't hesitate at the reading of "NOTHING BUT JOY" and wonder, "What?!!! How on earth is that even possible?" then perhaps you are further along the road of Christian maturity than I tend to find myself on most days. For indeed, James 1:3-4 goes on to say,

"...because you know that the testing of your faith produces endurance; and let endurance have its full effect, so that you may be mature and complete, lacking in nothing."

Each day is an opportunity to practice our faith and increase endurance so that we strive for the ultimate goal of growing into our complete selves, whole in the understanding that this journey has many twists and turns but God gives us his word to light our path, his love to surround us, his Son as our example, and the Holy Spirit to be our daily partner in real time.

As you read along in your Bible, I hope you enjoy coloring and making this book your own. I pray you will find yourself receiving the gift of wisdom that God intends for us when we let his Spirit work within us to live out these five chapters in the book of James.

James 1:1-4

"LORD, HELP ME BE A SERVANT TO YOU." (v1)

Sometimes, I forget I am here to live out your story (and not the other way around)

JOURNAL

Help me serve you daily and get my priorities straight

"TRIALS THEY WILL COME, BUT TAKE THEM AS JOY (v2)"

yes, JOY because whenever our faith is tested, it produces ENDURANCE & endurance works its full effect to make us MATURE

MATURE EQUALS COMPLETE & COMPLETE = LACKING NOTHING

IF we let our **FAITH** work within us, TRIALS DON'T MAKE US WEAKER, THEY MAKE OUR TRUST IN HIM **STRONGER**

THIS is what happens to a life lived in relationship with **GOD**

Here's *the* **THING** about **JOY:**

James isn't speaking here of how the world defines **JOY,**

NOT WORLD-GIVEN, WORLD-DEFINED, *fleeting,* CIRCUMSTANTIAL, DISTORTED.

BUT GOD-based ROCK SOLID ➡

FOUNDATIONAL JOY

RECEIVED WITH GOD'S *peace* (surpassing all understanding

WHICH RESULTS IN OUR SAYING *yes* to NOTHING but JOY

"The JOY of the LORD is my STRENGTH" Nehemiah 8:10

THINK of yourself as a BOAT

WHEN YOU WORRY YOUR PRAYERS,
IT'S LIKE YOU ARE SAILING ON
wind-whipped
waves

INSTEAD, when you come to God in prayer...

GO BOLDLY

Remember that your FATHER'S GREAT POWER + WISDOM

ANCHORING
yourself in God's
PROMISES, GRASPING IN
HIS LOVE FOR YOU,
ASSURED THAT COMES WHAT
MAY...

YOU ARE ANCHORED
TO GOD THE ROCK,
READY, STEADY, HELD
in all situations

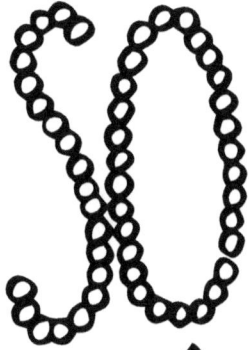

instead
GO HUMBLY
before your God,
giving him the
ultimate authority
in your own life
TRUE RICHES!!!

James 1:11

For WHEN WE CLING TO TEMPORARY *glories*

LIKE:

money
pride
popularity
success
beauty
talents
"FALSE GLORIES"
honors

WE ARE TEMPTED TO **HOLD TIGHTLY & NEVER LET THEM GO**

THE PROBLEM IS, THE **TIGHTER** OUR GRIP, THE MORE

all those things

START TO TAKE OVER AND REPLACE

GOD'S GLORY

in our hearts

THIS LEAVES US "POOR IN SPIRIT"

THAT'S WHY

WE ASK JESUS to help us

WE NEED JESUS TO HELP US LET GO of our false sense of CONTROL

Step 2 & Stop DEFINING

WHO WE ARE

BY

WHAT WE HAVE

...and STORE ...by the TRUE RICHES of GOD'S GLORY ... KINGDOM

When we get right down to it, human beings are WEAK and not always able to resist temptations. GOD KNOWS THIS

That's why God sent Jesus. ♪ "I am weak but He is strong." ♪

JESUS TAUGHT US TO PRAY: "Lead us not into temptation, but deliver us from evil."

Prayer

PRAYER is a "HELP-FULL" SHIELD because it grows our relationship with God & builds our lives around JESUS

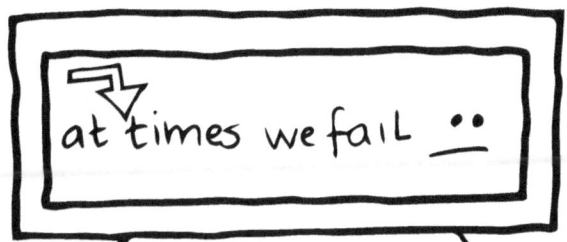

at times we fail ☹

we are more than HUMAN BEINGS we are "HUMANS DOING" (and we mess up)

READ Hebrews 4:14-16 & ♪ "Take it to the Lord in prayer" ♪

Take the mercy and accept the HELP (Hebrews 4:16)

ALL

GOOD THINGS COME FROM GOD

We LIVE IN A WORLD OF CONTRASTS

good/evil   LOVE/hate   LIGHT/DARK

LET YOUR heart FOCUS FOR a moment ON GOD as "THE FATHER OF LIGHT..."

The CREATOR OF THE Heavens created Y-O-U as a "CHILD OF LIGHT"

YOU are a SPARK FROM THE FATHER'S OWN LIGHT

THAT spark LIVES TO CONNECT TO ITS ORIGINAL SOURCE

GOD
YOU

You are GIVEN THE FREEDOM TO CHOOSE WHETHER you will CONNECT YOURSELF BACK TO HIS WORD of TRUTH

OR → LISTEN TO WHAT THE WORLD says

you choose

THE WORLD WILL TELL YOU:

"This is true" OR "That is true" OR "Who cares?" OR "Why does it matter?"

and the world's answers → are always CHANGING

BUT GOD STAYS the SAME & HIS WORD of TRUTH NEVER CHANGES

(never never never never never never never never never never never never)

Here's a BRIGHT idea

EVERY MORNING, wake-up & say a prayer, reconnecting yourself to your original source: GOD, THE FATHER OF LIGHT, SO YOU WILL GO THROUGH YOUR DAY ALIGHT WITH God's truth

(AND NOT THE WORLD'S)

HEARING & DOING

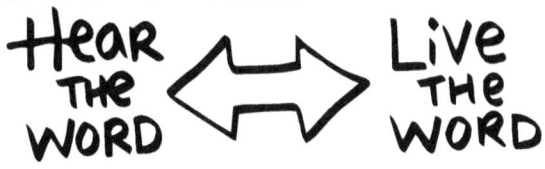

Hear the WORD ⟷ Live the WORD

The Bible says, "You must understand this, my beloved:"

"BE QUICK 2 LISTEN

BE SLOW 2 SPEAK

BE SLOW 2 ANGER"

When we are SLOW to listen, QUICK to speak, QUICK to anger, we behave in a way that blocks God's character from being evident in our actions

So what can help us do better?

HOLY BIBLE ← God's word is meant to be read & applied

WHEN WE READ PRAY APPLY God's word of truth in our lives, it becomes like a seed of truth planted in our hearts and we grow into more than HEARERS that can be easily deceived

God's Spirit invites us and guides us to participate in HIS STORY as DOERS living in relationship with HIM, seeking HIS kingdom & HIS righteousness.

Happy Day!

James 1:23-26

HEARING/DOING

James compares this to looking in a mirror ... STANDING DIRECTLY IN FRONT OF it, we have a CLEAR REFLECTION.

BUT as soon as we move away, we NO LONGER see the same REFLECTION

✝ JESUS mirrors > GOD

AND WE WANT TO STAY CLOSE TO HIM SO OUR ACTIONS MIRROR JESUS' ways

the goal HERE is NOT to look in the MIRROR & see our imperfect selves,

but the PERFECT LAW as represented by JESUS

FOCUSING in on our relationship with Jesus creates a Desire WITHIN US TO FOLLOW THROUGH ON what we learn in THE BIBLE

and GOD blesses our DOINGS

(see 2 Peter 1:3-11)

RELIGION
→ IS A WORD THAT HAS A MULTITUDE OF IDEAS & A LONG HISTORY BEHIND IT.

HERE, JAMES IS SPEAKING ABOUT RELIGION AS THE OUTWARD EXPRESSION OF HOW GOD WANTS US TO WORSHIP HIM.

WORSHIP GOES WAY BEYOND WHAT WE DO IN OUR CHURCHES ON SUNDAYS & HOW WE DO IT.

WORSHIP MUST CONTINUE WHEN WE WALK OUT THOSE DOORS & INTO THE WORLD. WORSHIP IS DEMONSTRATED DAILY THROUGH KINDNESSES THAT EXTEND BEYOND OUR LOVE FOR GOD TO LOVING & CARING FOR OTHERS

However, WHEN WE GO OUT INTO THE WORLD TO SHARE GOD'S LOVE,

WE MUST TAKE CARE THAT WE DON'T LET THE WORLD

DISTORT or distract or disengage US

FROM Serving IN A WAY THAT HONORS GOD

When we WORSHIP --- SERVE --- HONOR GOD outwardly,

IN SO DOING, WE INVITE OTHERS TO RECEIVE GOD'S LOVE INWARDLY

James 2:1-7

NO LABELS

WARNING against PARTIALITY!

We HAVE TO FIGHT AGAINST ANY TEMPTATION TO JUDGE PEOPLE BASED ON OUTWARD APPEARANCES OR LIMITED UNDERSTANDING

You are a clown

Actually, I'm an accountant

When we TREAT PEOPLE DIFFERENTLY BASED ON OUR OWN PERSONAL OPINIONS, OUR THINKING MAGNIFIES

OUR WORLDLY WAY AND NOT JESUS' WAY

LABELS DIVIDE ÷

CHRIST UNIFIES → ☰ ←

FOR THOUGH WE PRAY "in Jesus' name," we must also LIVE in Jesus' name

WHEN WE LIVE IN HIS NAME, OUR IDEAS ABOUT PEOPLE ARE FILTERED THROUGH THE HOLY SPIRIT AND WE DEVELOP A STRONG DESIRE TO Live & Love HIS WAY

MERCY

James 2:8-13

We ALL need it ...24 HRS a Day

At our BEST we remember to live out "LOVING our NEIGHBOR as OURSELF" more OFTEN we fail

Don't think of God's law as impossible: think of it as a life PATH He's set before us

"THIS is THE WAY, WALK-IN-IT" —Isaiah 30:21

We can choose God's pathway, or not, but we cannot pick & choose from God's laws

"For God will NOT be honored with exceptions" —Calvin

As people who have failed (often) & received mercy (abundantly), we are called to both → speak & ACT (continually) towards others with full acknowledgment that they are as needful of mercy as we are.

"Mercy triumphs over judgment" (v13)

James 2:14-26

Faith
WITHOUT WORKS is dead
(v17)

R.I.P.

Our faith
GOES BEYOND A SIMPLE STATEMENT OF WHAT WE BELIEVE—

AND IT WASN'T MEANT TO BE an INNER IDEA we CARRY AROUND INSIDE & BRING OUT AT OUR CONVENIENCE

FAITH

When we **ACTIVATE** our faith with **WORKS/DEEDS** ♥ ACTS of ♥ LOVINGKINDNESS, it COMES TO **LIFE!**

AND BECOMES AN ACTIVE

FAITH

an OUTER EXPRESSION OF AN INWARD RELATIONSHIP WITH FATHER, SON & HOLY SPIRIT.

In so DOING, OUR faith GROWS

and we GROW

FAITH WORKS

A WORKING FAITH CREATES A LIVING STRUCTURE THAT INVITES FATHER, SON & HOLY SPIRIT TO ENERGIZE WHAT WE DO & HOW WE LIVE DAY TO DAY

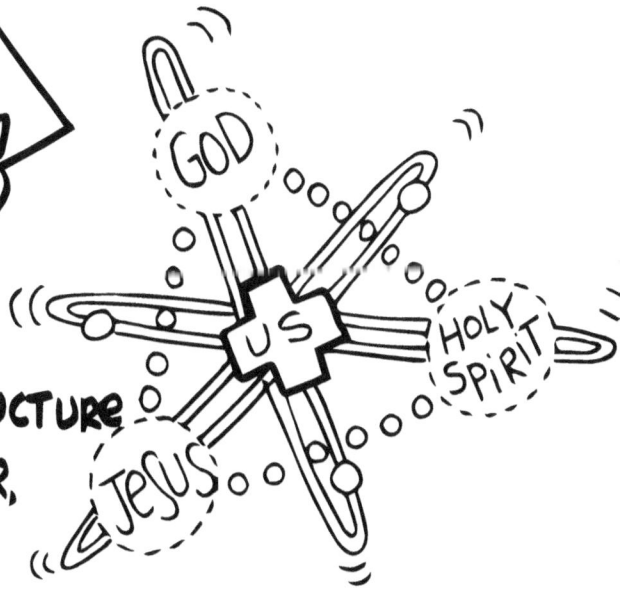

GOD

US

HOLY SPIRIT

JESUS

We as GOD'S CHILDREN, WHO LOVE HIM & RECEIVE HIS LOVE, ARE GUIDED BY OUR FAITH IN CHRIST JESUS

WHICH IS THEN

LIVED OUT DAILY WITH OUR "PARTNER IN TIME" the Holy Spirit

WHO WORKS WITHIN US TO CREATE A LIFE GREATER THAN WE COULD EVER ACCOMPLISH ON OUR OWN

FRIEND of GOD

The SCRIPTURE (GOD'S WORD) IS FULFILLED IN US AS IT WAS IN Abraham WHEN WE KEEP GROWING & LIVING OUT OUR FAITH IN ACTS OF LOVING-KINDNESS. EVEN AS Abraham WAS CALLED "FRIEND of GOD." SO WE CAN CALL OURSELVES AS WELL. Selah!

Taming of the Tongue

James 3:1-12

WORDS are POWERFUL

"AND ALL OF US make many mistakes" (v2)

WORDS aren't like kites—

—you can't PULL THEM BACK IN once they are SPOKEN

LIKE a HORSE GUIDED BY ITS BRIDLE OR a SHIP BY ITS RUDDER, THE WORDS THAT COME OUT OF OUR MOUTH DIRECT HOW WE "DO OUR DAY" (AND LONG-TERM, HOW WE "DO OUR LIFE"). FOR SUCH a SMALL BODY PART, OUR TONGUE is a POWERFUL INFLUENCE ON BOTH OUR ACTIONS & EMOTIONS.

The Words we CHOOSE

- can BUILD-UP OR TEAR DOWN
- can ENRICH OR POISON
- can HELP OR HURT

(both OURSELVES & OTHERS)

"From the same mouth comes blessing and cursing" (v10)

CONTROL

IT MAY BE NO SMALL TASK TO TAME THE TONGUE, BUT WE GO A **LONG WAY** IN GROWING OUR FAITH WHEN WE APPLY DISCIPLINED, SCRIPTURE-BASED PRAYER IN MANAGING OUR TONGUES

Psalm 141:3 Proverbs 18:21 Psalm 19:14 & THE **BEST** REASON TO KEEP OUR TONGUES IN TRAINING:

"For there is not a word on my tongue, but behold, O Lord, you know it altogether." Psalm 139:4

...when we humble ourselves before the MIGHTY HAND of GOD, acknowledging HIS AUTHORITY over us,

HE GIVES US GREATER grace

TO: YOU
FROM: GOD

THIS GREATER Grace permeates our spirit & enriches our relationship with GOD

DRAW near to GOD & HE WILL DRAW NEAR TO YOU (v8)

EACH NEW DAY WE HAVE THE OPPORTUNITY TO CHOOSE

HUMILITY & CLOSENESS WITH GOD

OR?

RELIANCE & GLORIFICATION OF SELF

THOSE WHO SEEK HIM

THOSE WHO HUMBLE THEMSELVES

FIND HIM

ARE LIFTED UP by his unending GRACE

EVERY STEP WE TAKE TOWARD GOD PULLS US INTO THE GLORIES OF A CLOSER RELATIONSHIP WITH OUR HEAVENLY FATHER & A LIFE BLESSED BY HIS PRESENCE ⇒ There is NOTHING better!!

James 4:11-12

WARNING
against JUDGING another
(BECAUSE WE NEED FREQUENT REMINDING)

WE MUST NOT SET OURSELVES UP AS JUDGE (OR JURY) OF WHO IS FOLLOWING GOD'S TEACHING & WHO IS NOT

1 THERE'S ONLY ONE BOSS, LAWGIVER & JUDGE (and you are not it)

WHILE WE ARE ON THIS EARTH, OUR JOB IS TO LOVE GOD & then to LOVE GOD'S PEOPLE

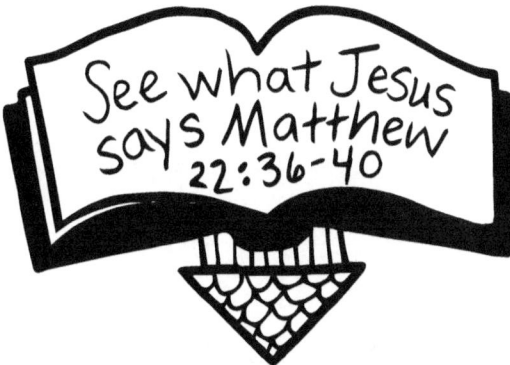

See what Jesus says Matthew 22:36-40

THIS IS FOUNDATIONAL TO a LIFE BUILT AROUND LOVING and SERVING GOD

JUDGING gets in the way of LOVING OTHERS

FOR we have ALL SINNED & FALLEN SHORT OF THE GLORY OF GOD

True

Romans 3:23

TO DO:
• LOVE GOD
• LOVE OTHERS

BOASTING ABOUT TOMORROW

BRAGGING ABOUT OUR FUTURE SUCCESS + REMOVES GOD FROM OUR PLANS.

OUR PLANS

DISCONNECTED FROM GOD'S WILL...

WILL NEVER HIT THE MARK

"To PLAN this way is to SIN. (v16-17)

"You do not even know what tomorrow will bring. What is your life?" (v14)

LIFE IS uncertain

WE DON'T KNOW HOW OUR STORIES WILL UNFOLD...

BUT WHEN WE REMOVE a PRACTICE OF BRAGGING AT THE GODLY WISHES, WE WILL HAVE GOD THIS FOR THAT (v16)

GOD'S WILL

MATTHEW 6:33

God places our hearts... He gives us paths... He maintains sleep...

Mis-placed treasures

James 5:1-6

"come now you rich people" (v1)

Putting too much value and importance on making money and letting it become the center of our existence and purpose, gives us a FAT heart

Wealth is an expert deceiver

We easily confuse being rich as the KEY to happiness in our lives to the point which we stop seeing the suffering & need going on around us

and a FATTENED HEART (v5) WILL NOT WORK PROPERLY

Just as a fattened heart results in narrowed arteries, a heart that is "spiritually fat" results in a narrow way of living, a way that no longer feels a need to connect to God as its life support

A healthy heart

Looks at the need & suffering around it and reacts with compassion, moved by the Holy Spirit,

Lord, "create in me a (c)Lean heart willing!" (Psalm 51:10)

James 5:7-11

patience IN SUFFERING

BUT HOW?

"BE PATIENT BELOVED" (v7)

(NO MATTER THE CIRCUMSTANCES)

(v8) "STRENGTHEN your hearts"

ALONG WITH KEEPING OUR HEARTS *LEAN*, WE MUST ALSO KEEP THEM STRONG BY PRACTICING

ENDURANCE

The Greek word for endurance is: **MAKROTHYMIA**

= "DIVINELY REGULATED PATIENCE" (v10)

(NOT PATIENCE THAT WE HAVE (OR DON'T HAVE) BUT PATIENCE THAT IS GIVEN BY GOD)

RELIANCE ON GOD

strengthens our *hearts* AND HELPS US SEE CLEARLY

---

patience & TRUSTING IN GOD'S purpose

IS ONE OF THE MOST CHALLENGING THINGS OUR FAITH CALLS US TO DO

BUT WE DO IT

BECAUSE WHEN WE HAVE FORMED A STRONG BOND & RELATIONSHIP WITH GOD, WE UNDERSTAND

THE LORD IS COMPASSIONATE & MERCIFUL

AND WORTHY OF OUR FULL FAITH & TRUST (Thank you, Lord!)

James 5:12
"Speaking your faith:"
consider your words
THINK CAREFULLY ABOUT THE WAYS YOU ADD UNNECESSARY EMPHASIS TO YOUR WORDS...
I swear!
I promise!
TRYING TO MANIPULATE OTHERS (AND GOD) WITH YOUR WORDS BY SWEARING, DEMONSTRATES A LACK OF FAITH
I swear to God!
NOT GOOD
WHEN YOU FEEL THE DEPTH OF GOD'S LOVE FOR YOU, USING HIS NAME IN VAIN SHOULD NEVER FEEL RIGHT COMING OUT OF YOUR MOUTH.
Instead of Swearing,
Jesus said
"SIMPLY LET YOUR YES BE 'YES' AND YOUR NO BE 'NO'"
(v12)
YES
NO
'YES' BOX
'NO' BOX
YOUR WORDS GIVING EVIDENCE OF THE CHARACTER AND INTEGRITY BEHIND YOUR FAITH - SEEMS PRETTY SIMPLE... yes or no?

James 5:13-18

The prayer of FAITH

THROUGH THESE FIVE CHAPTERS, James HAS BEEN PICKING UP a THREAD AND WEAVING IT THROUGH OUR DAY TO DAY LIVES & RELATIONSHIPS AND He's TiED iT ALL TOGETHER WiTH a FiNAL KNOT:

SORROWS
joys FAMILY CHURCH
PRAY aBOUT iT aLL!
SiNS
FAILURES
SiCKNESS SUCCESS WORK
DOUBTS RELATIONSHIPS
LiFE THE FUTURE
ACTIONS

prayer PULLS iT TOGETHER

FOR (v16)"...THE PRAYER OF THE RiGHTEOUS iS POWERFUL & EFFECTiVE."

James 5:19-20

Straying from the truth

We have all sinned and struggled along the way...

We lose our way
We get distracted
We doubt
We sin

Our faith journey

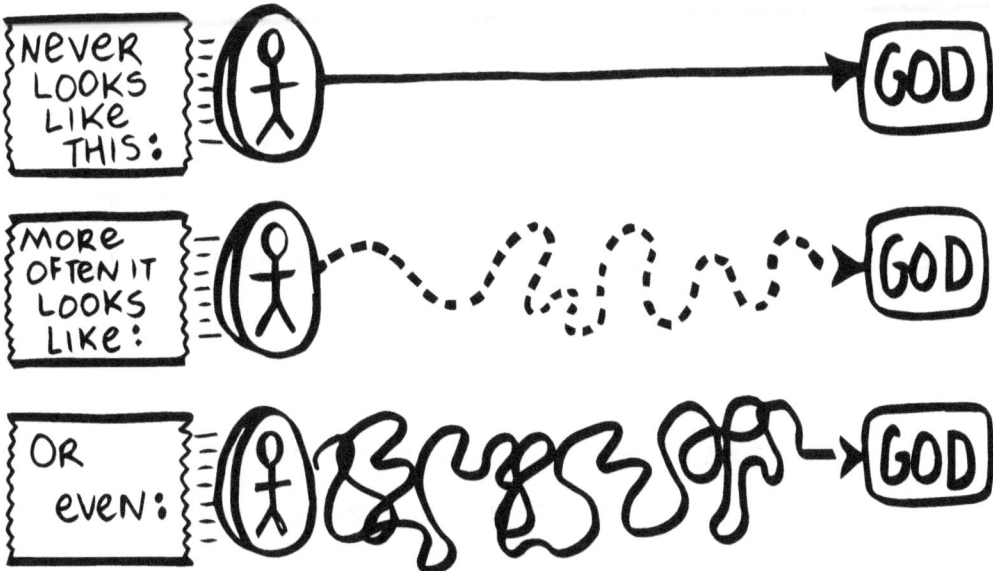

NEVER LOOKS LIKE THIS: → GOD

MORE OFTEN IT LOOKS LIKE: → GOD

OR EVEN: → GOD

AND we should count it as a blessing when a brother or sister in Christ loves us enough to come alongside us, point out our loss of direction, and offer us guidance. *Likewise*, we may be called to do the same for another.

ECCLESIASTES 4:9-10

"2 are better than one because they have a good return for their labor: [IF] either of them falls down, one can help the other up. But pity anyone who falls down & has no one to help them up."

EPILOGUE

The Prayer of Faith

At first, I was a little let-down at this abrupt, less than glossy ending to the book of James. I know that sounds contrary to judge a book of the Bible this way (or perhaps it sounds pretty typical of our culture today: "I want a big ending!") I prayed about my response to the ending. Enter the Holy Spirit whom I imagined whispering in my ear, "Oh, sorry it doesn't work for what you want to do with your book." And so I prayed, asking, "What am I missing?" Reading the end of James, I was definitey thinking, "What? That's it?!"

My response is a good example of why each of us is called to work our way through the Bible...no one can do it for you!! Realizing that we are never finished reading and learning from the Bible is one of the things that excites me the most about reading it. I take it as joy that I will never be done allowing it to challenge, shape and grow my faith... nor should you.

> "Open my eyes, so that I may behold wondrous things out of your law."
> ~Psalm 119:18 (NRSV)

It takes a lot of praying to get yourself through any Bible reading and that's what it took me to reach a resolution when it came to questions I had as to the ending of James chapter five. Months later, I looked at it again and it seemed so obvious --- PRAYING!!

James' final thought for us is that it all comes together with prayer and none of it ever comes together without prayer - both as inidividuals and as groups. Prayer is how God reaches us and grows our relationship with him.

In closing, I hope you've enjoyed this sharing of my studies of the book of James, but I certainly don't have all the answers. Christian maturity is a process, not a final product and I'm still in that process. Aren't we all? It is my hope that this study of James encourages others to develop a relationship with God which involves a whole lot of learning from Christ's example, his Word, and living out what his love looks like in life and in this world when we allow the Holy Spirit to shape and give direction to our lives and our relationships.

I'm still praying and learning about what "count it all as joy" looks like as I try to act it out in my own life. One thing I know for sure, it's not something anyone can do by themselves. I hope that has been made clear in this little book because there is nothing God would like better on a daily basis than to have you ask him for guidance and wisdom to apply his abundant joy to your own life!

Dedicated to those who set an example for me
of the JOY that comes from studying
and applying the Living Word.

morninggloriesandgraces.com

TRUE STRENGTH comes from
believing, "Lord, I am weak
but you are STRONG"

ROAR!

For the Good Shepherd
carries his lambs in his arms,
close to his heart   Isaiah 40:11

If you would like to see more art by Mary J. DuVal,
(who thanks you from the bottom of her heart for supporting her
creative adventures)
please visit
http://morninggloriesandgraces.blogspot.com
or
http://pbandjoyly.blogspot.com/